FARM TRACTORS

by Kristin L. Nelson

Lerner Publications Company • Minneapolis

To Grandpa Calvert, who spent his childhood riding tractors on his family's Iowa farm.

Text copyright © 2003 by Kristin L. Nelson

This book is available in two editions:
Library binding by Lerner Publications Company, a division of Lerner Publishing Group
Soft cover by First Avenue Editions, an imprint of Lerner Publishing Group
241 First Avenue North
Minneapolis, MN 55401 U.S.A.

Website address: www.lernerbooks.com

Library of Congress Cataloging-in-Publication Data

Nelson, Kristin L.
        Farm tractors / by Kristin L. Nelson.
            p.   cm. — (Pull ahead books)
        Includes index.
        Summary: Describes how tractors work and the different
    jobs they do on a farm.
        ISBN: 0–8225–0690–4 (lib. bdg. : alk. paper)
        ISBN: 0–8225–0607–6 (pbk. : alk. paper)
        1. Farm tractors—Juvenile literature. [1. Tractors.
    2. Agricultural machinery.] I. Title. II. Series.
    S711 .N38 2003
    631.3'72—dc21   2001005910

Manufactured in the United States of America
1 2 3 4 5 6 — JR — 08 07 06 05 04 03

What kind of machine has big, bumpy tires like this one?

Farm tractors have tires with bumpy
ridges. Ridges help tractors drive over
rocky ground and mud without slipping.

Tractors spend most days in the dirt.
They help farmers do many jobs.

A farmer controls a tractor with a **steering wheel.** The steering wheel makes a tractor turn.

This farmer sits in a **cab** to steer his tractor. A cab has windows on the front and on each side.

In front of the cab are small, round parts that help farmers see in the dark. Can you name them?

These parts are **headlights.** They make light so farmers can work at night.

3 1833 04303 0706

A tractor has another part that helps farmers work. On the back of a tractor is a **hitch.**

A hitch hooks up the tractor to machines that do many jobs.

Some machines help make the ground
ready for planting. This tractor pulls a
plow. The blades of the plow dig into
the dirt, then turn it over.

Plowed dirt is lumpy. The tractor pulls a harrow. Round blades cut through the lumps.

Next, the farmer hitches a seed drill to the tractor. Blades make holes in the dirt.

Then the drill drops seeds into the holes and covers them with dirt. What happens to seeds after they are planted?

Sun and rain help seeds grow. The seeds in this field have grown into tall corn plants.

A tractor works with a combine to cut and gather the corn. This is called **harvesting.**

These string beans are harvested by a
tractor that pulls a bean picker. The
picker has skinny metal fingers that
gather the beans.

Workers pack the string beans into boxes. The beans are ready to go to the grocery store.

Here is another harvesting job. This tractor pulls a mower to cut grass.

Next, a giant rake turns over the cut grass. The grass dries quickly in the sun. It becomes hay.

The tractor tows a baler through the field. It collects the hay and rolls it into big bales.

Farmers feed hay to farm animals.
What animals do you see here?

Tractors have other jobs, too. This
tractor uses a big shovel to clean up
the barn.

This tractor cuts a lawn. Can tractors
be used for fun, too?

Yes! This tractor is taking children for a hayride in a trailer.

Tractors plant seeds and harvest crops. They pull plows and trailers. Tractors are the most useful machines on a farm.

Facts about Farm Tractors

- Farm tractors help do many jobs besides the ones shown in this book. They can pull machines that chop weeds, stack bales of hay, and spray crops to keep bugs away.

- A farm tractor gets its power from an engine. Before engines were invented, most farm machines were pulled by horses.

- Some people collect old farm tractors for fun. A very old, rare tractor can be worth thousands of dollars!

- Another fun hobby is tractor pulling. Pullers fix up their tractors to be powerful. Then they have a contest to see which tractor can pull a heavy weight the farthest.

Parts of a Farm Tractor

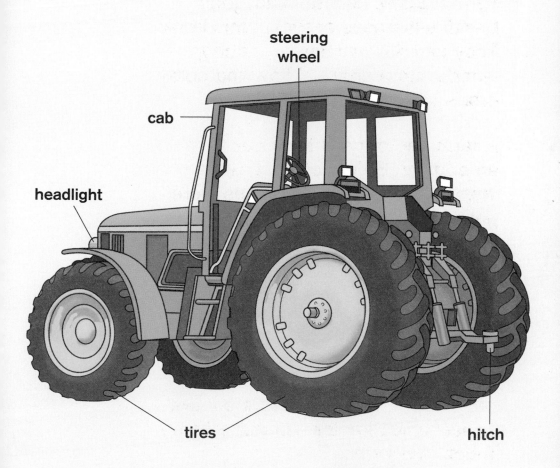

steering wheel

cab

headlight

tires

hitch

Glossary

cab: the part of a tractor where the driver sits. A cab has windows on each side.

harvesting: collecting crops from a field

headlights: lights on the front of a tractor

hitch: a hook on the back of a tractor that connects it to farm machines

steering wheel: a round tractor part that turns the tractor's wheels

Index

About the Author

Kristin L. Nelson loves writing books for children. Along with farm tractors, she has written about monster trucks and several animals for Lerner's Pull Ahead series. When she's not working on a book, Kristin enjoys reading, walking, and spending time with her four-year-old son, Ethan, and her husband, Bob. She and her family live in Savage, Minnesota.

Photo Acknowledgments

The photographs in this book appear courtesy of: © John Deere Photo Library, front cover, back cover, pp. 3, 4, 5, 6, 7, 8, 9, 10, 11, 12, 14, 15, 17, 20, 21, 22, 27, 31; © David Lorenz Winston, pp. 13, 16, 18, 19, 23, 24, 25; © Paul A. Souders/CORBIS, p. 26. Illustration on p. 29 by Laura Westlund, © Lerner Publications Company.